Mel Bay Presents

Hymns & Sacred Melodies for RECORDER

by William Bay

Hymns and Sacred Melodies for Recorder is an exciting collection of favorite Christian hymns arranged specifically for recorder performance. All of the hymns are voiced in the standard keys and harmonizations found in most hymnals. Therefore, the recorders may be used interchangeably with congregational singing in worship. The voicing is flexible. Soprano and alto parts are included. If one soprano and one alto recorder are used, the recommended voicing is to have the soprano recorder play the melody and the alto recorder play the alto harmony line. If several sopranos and altos are used, a desired voicing may still be to utilize the sopranos on the melody and the altos together on the alto harmony line. Another alternative voicing is to utilize the instrumentation exactly as written. In this case, the soprano recorders would divide between the melody and harmony parts, and the alto recorders would divide between the melody and harmony parts. It is hoped that this text will enable the recorder to be used effectively and creatively in worship.

1 2 3 4 5 6 7 8 9 0

© 1985 BY MEL BAY PUBLICATIONS, INC., PACIFIC, MO.
INTERNATIONAL COPYRIGHT SECURED. ALL RIGHTS RESERVED. PRINTED IN U.S.A.

Hymns and Sacred Melodies for Recorder

Title	Page
All Glory, Laud, and Honor	15
All Hail the Power of Jesus' Name	17
Alleluia, Sing to Jesus	24
Angels We Have Heard on High	34
Be Known to Us in Breaking Bread	4
Brethren, We Have Met to Worship	11
Christ the Lord Is Risen Today	36
Come, Christians, Join to Sing	8
Come, Thou Almighty King	20
Come Thou Fount	21
Come, Ye Faithful, Raise the Strain	37
Come, Ye Thankful People, Come	10
Come, Ye That Love the Lord	10
Coventry Carol	32
Crown Him with Many Crowns	14
Daily, Daily Sing the Praises	9
Divinum Mysterium	34
Doxology	3
Early Christmas Morn	30
Earth Is the Lord's (The)	27
Fairest Lord Jesus	12
Gloria Patri (Greatorex)	4
Gloria Patri (Meineke)	5
Glory Be to Jesus	7
God of Abraham Praise (The)	18
God Rest You Merry, Gentlemen	33
God the Omnipotent	14
He Is Risen	36
Holy God, We Praise Thy Name	15
Holy, Holy, Holy Lord God Almighty	13
Humbly I Adore Thee	19
Hymn to Joy	37
I Sing the Mighty Power of God	23
I Will Arise and Go to Jesus	25
Immortal, Invisible, God Only Wise	16
Jesus Calls Us	38
Jesus Shall Reign	22
Joy to the World	32
Lead On, O King Eternal	23
Let All Mortal Flesh Keep Silence	6
Lo, He Comes with Clouds Descending	31
Lord Bless You and Keep You (The)	5
Lord Our God Is Clothed with Might (The)	16
Lord, Speak to Me	6
Martyr Dei	19
Morning Song	26
My Faith Looks Up To Thee	39
Now Thank We All Our God	17
O Come, Creator Spirit	19
O Come, O Come, Emmanuel	30
O For a Thousand Tongues to Sing	13
O God, Our Help in Ages Past	24
O Master, Let Me Walk With Thee	21
O My Soul, Bless God the Father	12
O Sacred Head	35
On Jordan's Stormy Banks	26
Praise My Soul, The King of Heaven	28
Praise Round	27
Praise the Savior	9
Praise to the Lord, the Almighty	18
Rejoice, Ye Pure in Heart	7
Rosa Mystica	33
Solid Rock	28
Stand Up, Stand Up for Jesus	22
Strife Is O'er (The)	35
Tallis Canon	3
Thanksgiving Hymn	38
There Is a Balm in Gilead	29
Threefold Amen	3
We Three Kings	31
Welcome, Happy Morning	8
Were You There	29
When I Survey the Wonderous Cross	20
When Jesus Wept	25
Wonderous Love	11
Master Fingering Chart	40

Doxology
(Old 100th)

Tallis Canon

Threefold Amen

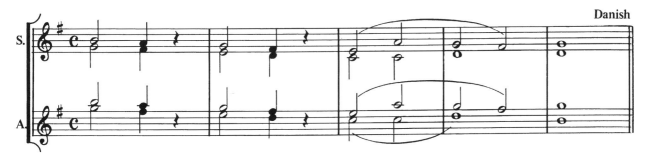

Gloria Patri

Greatorex 1813-1858

Be Known To Us In Breaking Bread
(St. Flavian)

From
John Day's Psalter 1562

The Lord Bless You and Keep You
(4 Part Harmony)

P. Lutkin

Gloria Patri

Meineke 1782 - 1850

Let All Mortal Flesh Keep Silence
(Picardy)

17th Cent. French

Lord, Speak To Me
(Canonbury)

Robert Schuman 1810-1856

Glory Be To Jesus
(Caswall)

Friedrich Filitz, 1847

Rejoice, Ye Pure In Heart
(Marion)

Arthur Messiter 1883

Welcome, Happy Morning
(Hermas)

Francis Havergal 1836 - 1879

Come, Christians, Join To Sing
(Spanish Hymn)

Spanish Hymn

Daily, Daily, Sing The Praises

William Bay

© 1980 by Mel Bay Publications, Inc. All Rights Reserved.

Praise The Savior

German Melody

Come, Ye That Love The Lord
(St. Thomas)

Aaron Williams 1731-1776

Come, Ye Thankful People, Come
(St. George's Windsor)

George Elvey 1816-1893

Brethren, We Have Met To Worship
(Holy Manna)

William Moore
in "Colombian Harmony" 1825

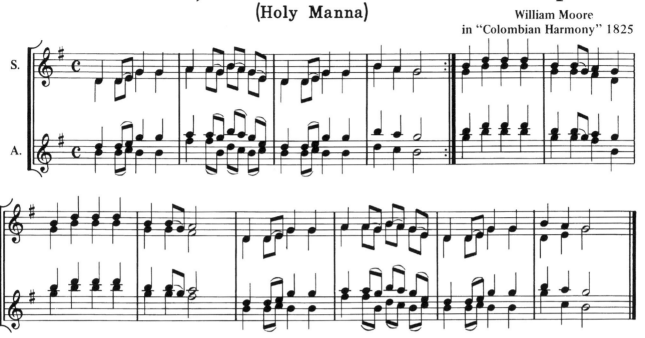

Wondrous Love

Southern Harmony, 1835

O My Soul, Bless God The Father
(Stuttgart)

Henny Gauntlett 1805 - 1876

Fairest Lord Jesus
(St. Elizabeth)

Schlesische Volkslieder, 1842

Holy, Holy, Holy I Lord God Almighty
(Nicaea)

John B. Dykes 1873 - 1876

O For A Thousand Tongues To Sing

Carl Gläser

Crown Him With Many Crowns
(Diademata)

George Elvey 1816 - 1893

God The Omnipotent
(Russian Hymn)

Alexis Lvov 1798 - 1870

All Glory, Laud, And Honor
(St. Theodulf)

Melchior Teschner 1584 - 1635

Holy God, We Praise Thy Name
(Grosser Gott)

Te Deum

1774

Immortal Invisible, God Only Wise
(St. Denio)

Welsh Melody

The Lord Our God Is Clothed With Might
(Detroit)

Early American
Supplement to Kentucky Harmony 1820

Now Thank We All Our God
(Nun Danket)

Johann Crüger 1598-1662

All Hail The Power Of Jesus' Name
(Coronation)

Oliver Holden 1765-1844

Praise To The Lord, The Almighty
(Lobe Den Herren)

Stralsund Gesangbuch - 1665

The God Of Abraham Praise
(Leoni)

Meyer Lyon 1751 - 1797

Come, Thou Almighty King
(Italian Hymn)

Felice De Giardini 1716 - 1796

When I Survey The Wondrous Cross
(Hamburg)

Ancient Chant

O Master, Let Me Walk With Thee
(Maryton)

H. Perry Smith 1825 - 1898

Come Thou Fount
(Nettleton)

American Folk Melody

Stand Up, Stand Up For Jesus
(Webb)

George Webb 1803 - 1887

Jesus Shall Reign
(Duke Street)

John Hatton 1793

Lead On, O King Eternal
(Lancashire)

Henry Smart 1813-1879

I Sing The Mighty Power Of God
(Ellacombe)

Gesangbuch der Herzogl, 1784

O God, Our Help In Ages Past
(St. Anne)

William Croft 1678 - 1727

Alleluia, Sing To Jesus
(Hyfrydol)

Roland Prichard 1811 - 1887

When Jesus Wept

I Will Arise And Go To Jesus

Morning Song

Wyeth's Sacred Music, 1813

On Jordan's Stormy Banks
(Promised Land)

American Folk Melody

The Earth Is The Lord's
(Psalm 24)

Round

William Bay

© 1984 by Mel Bay Publications, Inc. All Rights Reserved.

Praise Round

William Bay

© 1984 by Mel Bay Publications, Inc. All Rights Reserved.

The Solid Rock
(Solid Rock)

William Bradbury 1816 - 1868

Praise My Soul, The King of Heaven
(Lauda Anima)

John Goss, 1869

There Is A Balm In Gilead

Were You There

O Come, O Come, Emmanuel
(Veni Emmanuel)

Plainsong, Mode I

Early Christmas Morn

William Bay
13th Century Melody

© 1974 by Mel Bay Publications, Inc. All Rights Reserved.

We Three Kings
(Kings of Orient)

John Hopkins 1820 - 1891

Lo, He Comes With Clouds Descending
(Bryn Calfaria)

William Owen 1814 - 1893

Coventry Carol

Joy to the World
(Antioch)

God Rest You Merry, Gentlemen

Rosa Mystica

Michael Praetorius 1609

Divinum Mysterium

13th Century Plainsong Mode V

Angels We Have Heard On High
(Gloria)

French

O Sacred Head, Now Wounded
(Passion Chorale)

Hans Hassler

The Strife Is O'er

Palestrina, 1558

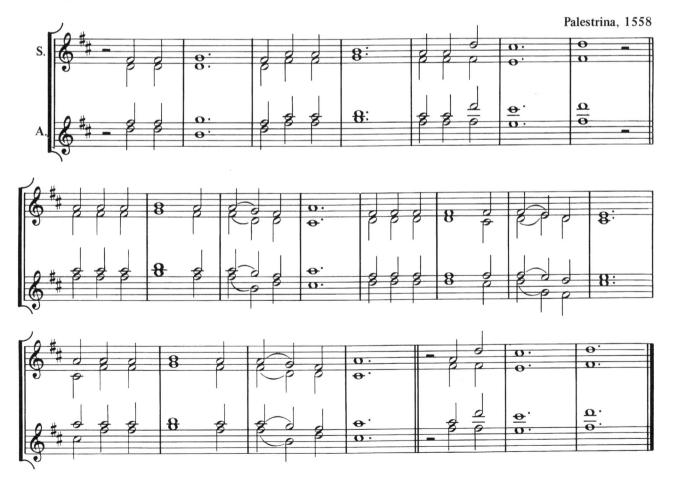

He Is Risen
(Neander)

Joachim Neander, 1680

Christ The Lord Is Risen Today
(Easter Hymn)

Come, Ye Faithful, Raise The Strain
(St. Kevin)

Arthur Seymour Sullivan 1872

Hymn To Joy

Beethoven

Jesus Calls Us
(Galilee)

William Jude 1851 - 1922

Thanksgiving Hymn
(Kremser)

My Faith Looks Up To Thee
(Olivet)

Lowell Mason 1792 - 1872

O Worship The King
(Lyons)

Michael Haydn 1737 - 1806

FINGERING CHART FOR THE MOST COMMON RECORDERS
WITH ALTERNATE FINGERINGS

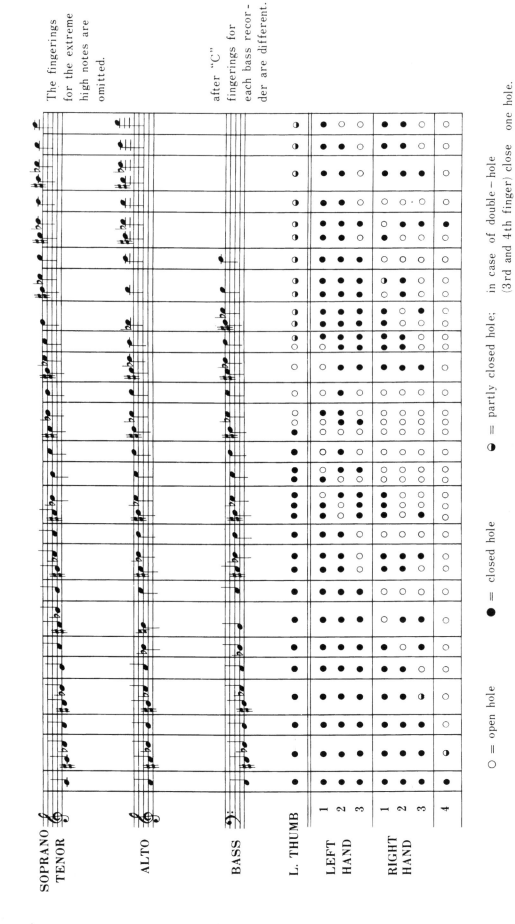

40

Made in the USA
Las Vegas, NV
13 February 2021